Animal Tricksters

Candy Gourlay

Illustrated by
Galia Bernstein
Margaret Chamberlain
Thomas Docherty

CONTENTS

OXFORD
UNIVERSITY PRESS

Dear Reader,

All over the world people tell stories about clever animals who trick their friends. Here are three very old stories about a hare from South Africa, a monkey from the Philippines and a coyote (wild dog) from North America.

I do hope you enjoy them,

Candy Gourlay

Hare Takes a Wife

A folk tale from South Africa

Hare was a good-looking fellow. It didn't take him long to find a lady hare who was happy to become his wife.

'Hare, dear,' said Mrs Hare, very soon after they were married, 'you should begin clearing this jungle so that you can grow some crops.'

'Of course, my sweet,' said Hare. 'I will have it cleared by sundown.'

'By sundown?' said Mrs Hare. 'It's so big and wide and long! How can you clear it all by then?'

'Trust me, my sweet,' said Hare. 'It will be cleared by sundown.'

Hare took a long rope and some tools and went into the jungle.

But Hare was as lazy as he was handsome. He didn't chop down trees and clear the scrub. Instead, he put down his tools and stretched. 'I think I need a little walk,' he yawned.

He took the rope and wandered through the jungle. Soon, he came upon Hippo. He was snoozing next to his mud hole.

'Hello, Hare,' called Hippo. 'How is married life?'

'It is wonderful,' said Hare. 'My new wife says I am the strongest animal in the jungle. And I have to say that she is right!'

'What?' said Hippo, annoyed. 'How can you say that? Everyone knows that the hippopotamus is the strongest animal in the jungle.'

'You?' Hare rolled his eyes. 'Why, I bet I can pull you over with this rope.'

Hippo laughed. Hare must be as stupid as he was vain.

'Go on then!' he said. 'I'll pull on one end while you pull on the other. Let's see who pulls the other one over first!'

So Hare gave Hippo one end of the rope. He took the other end through the trees to where Elephant was grazing.

'Hello, Hare,' called Elephant. 'How is
married life?'

'It is great,' said Hare. 'My new wife says
I am the strongest animal in the jungle. And
I have to say that she is right!'

'What?' Elephant said, annoyed. 'How can you say that? Everyone knows that the elephant is the strongest animal in the jungle.'

'You?' Hare rolled his eyes. 'Why, I bet I can pull you over with this rope.'

Elephant snorted. Hare must be as silly as he was stupid.

'Go on then!' he said. 'I'll pull on one end while you pull on the other. Let's see who pulls the other one over first!'

Hare gave the other end of the rope to Elephant. Then he went back through the trees to where the middle of the rope lay on the ground.

He gave it a mighty jerk. Elephant and Hippo, thinking that the contest had begun, pulled as hard as they could.

Backwards and forwards, from side to side, went the rope. Huge trees were tugged out by their roots. Everything in the way was crushed to the ground.

Hippo couldn't believe it. He had not expected Hare to be so strong. He pulled even harder.

Elephant was amazed. How could a small animal like Hare be so powerful?

They **pulled** and **pulled** ...

and **pulled** ...

At last the two of them fell down, tired out.

Hare strolled up to Hippo, dusting his hands. 'Well, that was fun,' he said.

Hippo gasped and panted on the ground. 'You win, Hare. You really are the strongest in the jungle. Your wife is very lucky.'

Hare ambled over to Elephant, stretching and yawning. 'I enjoyed that,' he said. 'Shall we do it again?'

Elephant groaned. 'I'm sorry I didn't believe you, Hare. You really are the strongest in the jungle. Your wife should be very proud of you.'

Hare showed Mrs Hare the land that Elephant and Hippo had cleared.

'I did as I promised, my sweet,' he said. 'I cleared it before sundown. I bet you didn't believe me.'

'Of course I believed you!' said Mrs Hare. 'In fact, I was so sure you would finish that I've invited some friends for dinner.'

'Friends for dinner, my sweet?' said Hare. 'Who have you invited?'

'Elephant and Hippo!' said Mrs Hare.
'I can't wait to show them how much
work you've done today.'

Monkey and Mango Island

It was said that Mango Island had the sweetest mangoes in the world. But Mango Island was in the middle of the world's deepest river ... and in the river lived the world's meanest crocodiles. Twenty of them.

No one could reach the delicious mangoes. What a waste!

One day, Monkey came to the riverbank with a big basket.

The crocodiles sniggered among themselves and snapped their jaws. 'What is the basket for, little one?' the biggest crocodile asked.

'I am off to gather mangoes on Mango Island,' Monkey replied.

'Ha!' said the biggest crocodile. 'If you try to cross the river, we twenty crocodiles will eat you up!'

'Twenty?' Monkey looked confused. 'There are only ten of you.'

'Stupid monkey!' the biggest crocodile roared. 'Can't you see there are twenty of us?'

Monkey shook his head. 'I don't know what you mean. I can only count ten.'

'WE ARE THE MEANEST CROCODILES IN THE WORLD!'

the biggest crocodile yelled.

'AND THERE ARE TWENTY OF US!'

'Look,' Monkey said. 'Why don't you line up and let me count you?'

The crocodiles lined up side by side. There were so many of them that they stretched all the way from the riverbank to Mango Island.

Monkey began to count. 'One, two, three, four, five ...' As he counted, Monkey stepped on the back of each crocodile, basket in hand. ' ... eighteen, nineteen, twenty!'

He hopped off the last one onto Mango Island. 'It is true, there are twenty of you!' he called as he scrambled up to the tops of the mango trees. 'Thank you! Now I can gather mangoes!'

The crocodiles realised that they had been tricked. 'You think you're so clever!' the biggest crocodile growled. 'But remember, you still have to go back to the riverbank. We'll be waiting for you.'

With that, the crocodiles started to swim around the island waiting for Monkey to finish gathering his mangoes.

By the time Monkey had filled his basket full of mangoes, the crocodiles had missed lunch and were very hungry. 'Mmm,' the biggest crocodile said, 'I can't wait to eat his liver. Monkey liver is my favourite food.'

'My liver?' Monkey said. 'Oh I'm sorry.
I left my liver on the riverbank, on the
Liver Tree.'

'What Liver Tree?' the biggest
crocodile said.

'All monkeys hang their livers up
to dry on the Liver Tree,' Monkey said.
'Do you want me to show
you where that is?'

'Oh yes, please,' the biggest crocodile said, licking his lips. He was pleased with himself. If Monkey took them to the Liver Tree, there would be more liver for all the crocodiles.

'If you let me ride on your back, we can get there more quickly,' Monkey said.

The biggest
crocodile held still
while Monkey climbed
onto his back with his basket
of mangoes.

'Just over there,' Monkey pointed to the riverbank.

The biggest crocodile swam to the riverbank and his crocodile brothers followed, smacking their lips at the thought of lunch at last.

But when they got to the riverbank, Monkey leaped off the biggest crocodile's back and scampered up a tall coconut tree.

The crocodiles realised that they had been tricked again. They crawled out of the water to the coconut tree, snapping their jaws in anger.

At that moment, Monkey's brothers and sisters peered through the leaves high up in the other coconut trees. They laughed and threw coconuts at the crocodiles until the crocodiles were forced back into the water.

'You're not going to get away with this!' the biggest crocodile roared as he swam away. 'We'll be waiting for you.'

Monkey didn't care. He and his brothers and sisters were busy eating mangoes.

And it was true. The mangoes of Mango Island *were* the sweetest in the world.

Coyote and Mountain Lion

A folk tale from North America

Coyote was minding her own business when she heard the sound of crying from behind a large rock.

Sob!

She went to have a look and who should she find but Mountain Lion, sitting down to supper.

'Well, hello Mountain Lion,' Coyote said.

'Well, hello Coyote,' Mountain Lion said. 'Please excuse me as I was just sitting down to eat.'

On Mountain Lion's plate were three baby rabbits. 'Oh please, Mister Mountain Lion, don't eat us!' the baby rabbits cried.

'Pardon me for saying so,' Coyote said,
'but those baby rabbits are the tiniest,
scrawniest, boniest baby rabbits that I have
ever seen.'

'I don't care,' Mountain Lion said.
'I'm starving.'

'You shouldn't settle for these bony bunnies,' Coyote said. 'Why, just past that cluster of rocks I saw a giant pumpkin and scratching and scraping inside it were ten of the fattest, juiciest baby bunnies I have ever seen.'

'Ten baby bunnies?' Mountain Lion said, licking his lips, for he was very greedy.

'Come with me and I will show you where they are!' Coyote ran off and Mountain Lion scrambled after her. The three baby bunnies clambered off the plate and ran home to their mothers.

Sure enough, just behind a cluster of rocks, there was a giant pumpkin. Mountain Lion sniffed at the pumpkin.

'I don't see any bunnies!' he growled.

'They're inside!' Coyote said. 'See that hole? I saw them go in through there.'

Mountain Lion pushed his head into the hole.

No bunnies.

Still no bunnies.

Then he tried to pull his head out.

He pulled and he pulled and he pulled ...
He was stuck fast.

'You tricked me!' Mountain Lion roared.

'I hope you like pumpkin,' Coyote laughed as she ran quickly up a mountain path, 'because you are going to have to eat your way out.'

But Mountain Lion swung the pumpkin against a rock and smashed it to pieces.

'Well, Coyote!' he yelled. 'Now I am going to have *you* for supper!'

Mountain Lion raced after Coyote. When he turned the corner, he was surprised to find Coyote holding up a cliff.

Mountain Lion was just about to grab her when Coyote cried, 'Don't be stupid, Mountain Lion! Can't you see that I'm holding up the cliff? If you grab me it will collapse and kill us both!'

'I'm hungry!' Mountain Lion roared. 'I'm going to have *you* for supper!'

'Well, you hold this and I will get a log to prop it up,' Coyote said. 'No point getting crushed by a cliff before supper.'

So Mountain Lion held up the cliff while Coyote scrambled off, down the path towards the lake.

It didn't take long before Mountain Lion realised that Coyote had tricked him again! The cliff wasn't going to fall at all.

Mountain Lion hurried after Coyote, yelling, 'You tricked me again! I'm having you for supper!'

When he got to the lake, Mountain Lion saw that Coyote had changed into a swimming costume.

He was just about to grab her when Coyote cried, 'Wouldn't you like some cheese with your supper?'

'Cheese?' Mountain Lion stopped. He was so hungry. Some cheese would make a nice second course.

Coyote pointed into the lake. There, shimmering at the bottom, was a huge wheel of yellow cheese.

'I was just going to dive in and get it for you,' Coyote said.

But Coyote had already tricked Mountain Lion twice and Mountain Lion wasn't going to let it happen again. 'You're just going to steal it!' he yelled, 'I am going to get it myself!'

Without a second thought, he leaped into the lake.

Of course when he got to the bottom he found nothing there. The wheel of cheese was just the full moon reflected in the water.

When Mountain Lion climbed out of the lake, shivering with cold, Coyote was nowhere to be seen.